Magnets

A FOLLETT BEGINNING SCIENCE BOOK

SCIENCE EDITOR:

EDWARD VICTOR, ED. D.
Professor of Science Education,
Northwestern University

Tested in the Evanston Public Schools by
JEANNE S. BROUILLETTE,
Curriculum Coordinator, Elementary Schools

Library of Congress Catalog Card Number: 62-8713

Edward Victor

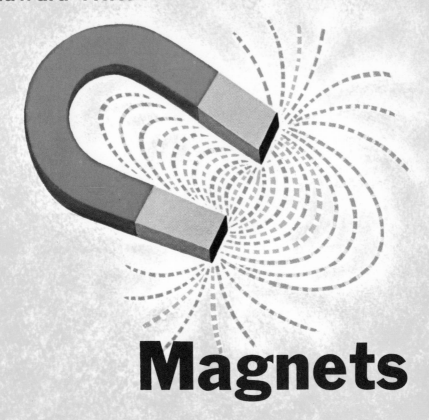

Magnets

Illustrated by William Sayles

Follett Publishing Company   **Chicago**

A magnet is fun to play with. It will pick up paper clips, iron nails and tacks, and steel wool that has been cut up with scissors.

A magnet will pick up needles and pins. It will even pick up the cover from a can.

But it will not pick up pieces of wood, paper, cloth, rubber, or glass.

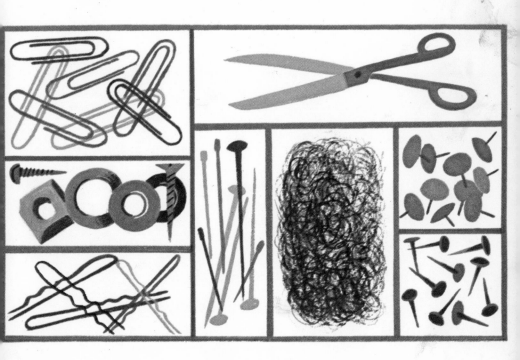

A magnet will pick up all kinds of
things, but only if they are made
of metal.

But a magnet will not pick up things
that are made of just any metal.

A magnet will pick up only the things
that are made of iron and steel.

There are two kinds of magnets. Some
magnets are made by man. There are also
natural magnets.

One of the natural magnets is found
in the ground. It is called lodestone. A
lodestone is a kind of rock that has iron
in it.

Lodestone is the first magnet that
man ever knew.

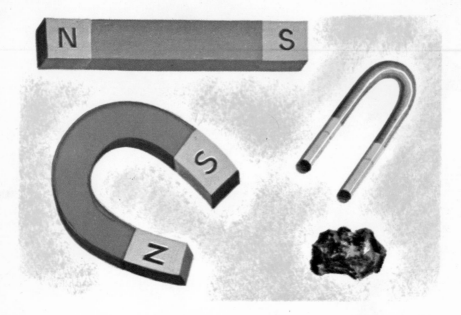

Most man-made magnets are made of iron
or steel. They can be made into many shapes.

Some are made straight. They are called
bar magnets. Others are shaped like the letter
U. Still others look like little horseshoes.

The little magnets in pot holders or on
bulletin boards are called Alnico magnets.
These are small and light, but they are very
strong.

A magnet will pull on pieces of iron and steel even without touching them. Bring a magnet near a steel tack. The magnet will pull, or attract, the tack to it.

Magnets attract through many things: air, paper, glass, wood, and aluminum.

Move a magnet underneath a glass pie plate. This will make paper clips inside the pie plate move.

But a magnet will not attract the clips if they are inside a plate with iron or steel in it.

The ends of a magnet are called its poles.
The pull of a magnet is strongest at its ends
or poles.

The magnet picks up things best at its
poles. Two poles close together pull more
than just one pole. A horseshoe magnet has
more pull than a bar magnet.

Every magnet has two poles. One pole
is called the north-seeking pole. The other
pole is called the south-seeking pole.

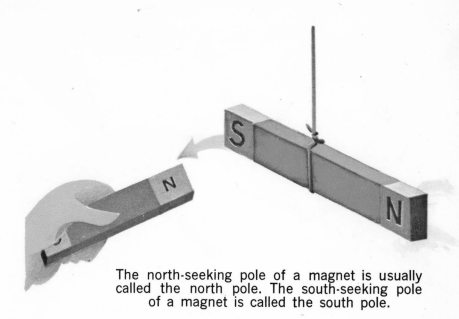

The north-seeking pole of a magnet is usually called the north pole. The south-seeking pole of a magnet is called the south pole.

If we bring the north-seeking pole of one magnet near the south-seeking pole of another magnet, the north-seeking pole will pull, or attract, the south-seeking pole to it.

The same thing happens when we bring a south-seeking pole of one magnet near the north-seeking pole of another magnet.

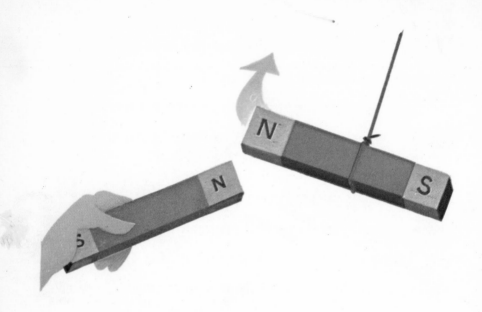

But a north-seeking pole of one magnet will push away, or repel, the north-seeking pole of another magnet.

And the south-seeking pole of one magnet will repel the south-seeking pole of another magnet.

Two different kinds of poles will pull, or attract, each other. And two of the same kind of poles will push away, or repel, each other.

We can show how a magnet will attract a paper clip without touching it.

Put a bar magnet underneath a piece of heavy white paper. Cut steel wool into small bits with a scissors.

Let the bits of steel wool drop all over the paper. Now tap the paper a few times.

The bits of steel wool will make a picture of the space around a magnet.

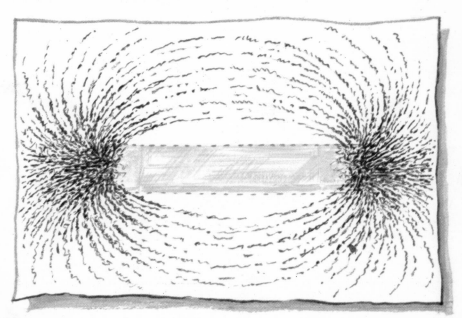

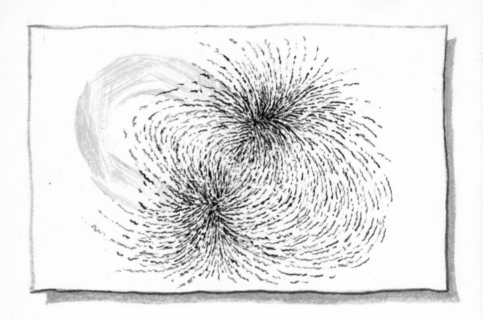

The space around a magnet is called
the magnetic field. As soon as a paper clip
comes into the magnetic field, it begins to
be attracted by the magnet.

Make a magnetic field for a horseshoe
magnet too. See how much more steel wool
there is at the poles of both magnets.

Magnets are strongest at the poles
and weakest in the middle.

When a magnet picks up an iron tack,
the tack becomes a magnet for a little while.
The tack can now pick up other tacks. The
other tacks become magnets too.

When the magnet is taken away, the tacks
are no longer magnets.

Things that become magnets for only a
little while are called temporary magnets.

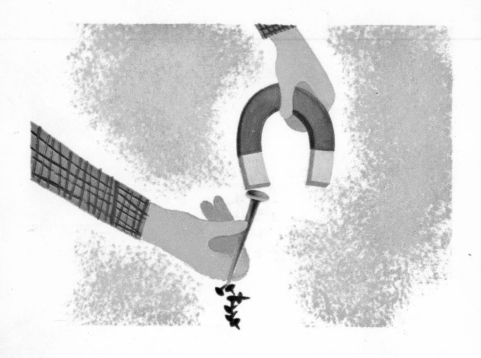

An iron nail can be made into a
temporary magnet just by bringing it very
near to a strong magnet. It will pick up
iron tacks or paper clips.

When the magnet is taken away, the
tacks and paper clips fall off. The nail
is not a magnet any more.

You can make your own magnet. Get a large iron nail. Rub the nail with one pole of a strong magnet.

Do not rub the magnet back and forth. Just rub it in one direction, and with only one pole of the magnet.

Rub the nail one way for fifty times. One hundred times is even better.

Now the nail is a magnet. Test the magnet you have made. It will pick up paper clips and tacks.

It is not as strong as the magnet that made it. But it is like a magnet in every way.

It has a north-seeking pole and a south-seeking pole. It has a magnetic field.

Put the nail away for a few days and
see what happens.

The nail will not pick up things any
more. It will have lost its magnetism. It
was only a temporary magnet.

The nail is made of iron. It is easy
to make magnets out of iron things. But
iron things lose their magnetism just as
easily.

Now let us make another magnet. This time
we will use a steel knitting needle. We will
have to rub the needle many more times than
we rubbed the nail.

But the needle will act like a magnet for
a long, long time. It will not lose its
magnetism. A magnet that does not lose its
magnetism is called a permanent magnet.

The needle is made of steel. It is harder
to make a magnet from steel things. But when
we do, the steel magnets are permanent ones.

We can make a magnet with electricity.
All we need is a large iron nail, a big dry
cell, and some bell wire. We can get these
things at the hardware store.

Wrap the bell wire around the nail
twenty-five times. Connect the ends of the
wires to the screws of the dry cell.

Be sure to take the cover off the ends
of the wires first, so they are bare.

The nail will now act like a magnet.
It is called an electromagnet.

An electromagnet that uses a nail is
a temporary magnet. It acts like a magnet
only as long as electricity from the dry cell
goes through the wire.

If we take one end of the wire away
from one of the screws on the dry cell, the
nail will no longer be a magnet.

But if we make an electromagnet with a
steel knitting needle, the steel needle will
become a permanent magnet.

Permanent magnets can become weak and lose their magnetism. If a magnet is dropped or hit with a hammer, it will become weak.

When two magnets are put away with the north-seeking poles or the south-seeking poles side by side, the magnets will become weak. They will not be able to pick up things.

Using a keeper helps to keep a magnet strong. A keeper is a small flat piece of iron. Put a keeper across the poles of a horseshoe magnet.

Put two bar magnets away with a north-seeking pole beside a south-seeking pole. Put a keeper across both poles.

If you have a bar magnet, let it hang
from a string.

Do not hang it near anything made of
iron or steel.

You will see the magnet swing a little.
Then it will come to a stop. The north-seeking
pole of the magnet will now point to the north.

This is why we call it a north-seeking
pole. The pole seeks, or looks for, the north.

A compass tells us which way is north.

A compass has a little magnet inside it.
The magnet can move around easily. We call
this magnet a compass needle.

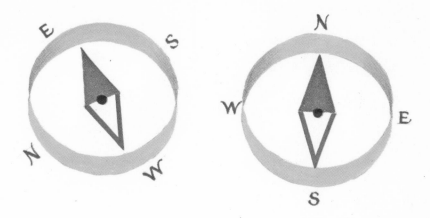

A compass works just like the bar magnet.
The little magnet in the compass swings around
until its north-seeking pole points to the north.

The swinging needle in a compass will
point to the north unless a strong magnet or
a lot of iron is near.

When you use a compass, you must always
turn the compass slowly around. Do this until
the dark end of the needle is over the letter N.

Now the dark end points to where north
is. Once you know where north is, you can
tell where east, south, and west are too.

When Columbus discovered America he used a simple floating compass. You can make one like it.

First make a magnet out of a sewing needle. Do this by rubbing it many times in one direction with one pole of a strong magnet.

Then push the needle through a flat piece of cork stopper, and put the cork in a dish of water.

The cork and needle will move around until one end of the needle points to the north. The other end points to the south.

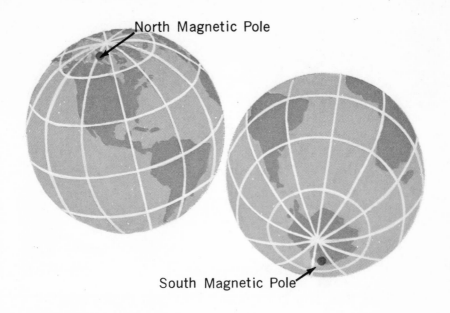

North Magnetic Pole

South Magnetic Pole

The swinging magnet in a compass points
to the north because the earth acts like a
very, very large magnet.

The magnetism of the earth makes the
north-seeking end of the magnet point to
the north.

Men on ships use compasses to know
where to go. Boy Scouts use compasses when
they are on a hike. Some people use a compass
in their automobile.

We use magnets for many things. All
electric motors need magnets to make them
work. Many of the machines we use in our
homes are run by electric motors.

Magnets help people do work in many
shops and factories, too.

Big electromagnets lift heavy loads of
iron and steel. These machines drop their
loads just where they are wanted as soon
as the electricity is turned off.

Magnets help us in so many ways that
we could not live as we do today without
magnets.

Words Younger Children May Need Help With
(Numbers refer to the page on which the word first appears.)

THINGS TO DO IN THE CLASSROOM OR AT HOME

Play a game with magnets. Get a lot of pins, tacks, screws, nuts, and bolts. Put them in a paper box. Make a fishing pole magnet. Get a long thin stick and tie a string around one end of the stick. Tie the other end of the string to the middle part of a horseshoe magnet. Now you and your friends can take turns fishing for the pins, tacks, screws, nuts, and bolts. A pin can be worth one point, a tack two points, a screw three points, a nut four points, and a bolt five points. After everyone has had a turn, count the number of points each has. Whoever has the most number of points wins the game.

Make a picture of a magnetic field. Get a piece of blueprint paper. Lay the paper on a piece of cardboard. Put a bar magnet underneath the cardboard. Cut fine steel wool into very tiny bits and sprinkle the steel wool over the cardboard. Tap the cardboard a few times to make a picture of the magnetic field.

Now bring the blueprint paper and cardboard over to the window and let the sunlight shine on it for a few minutes. Take the blueprint paper away from the sunlight and blow away the bits of steel wool. Wash the blueprint paper in water, then let it dry. You will now have a picture of a magnetic field.

Try some experiments with magnets. Some magnets do not have markings which tell you which is the north-seeking pole and which is the south-seeking pole. If you want to find out the poles of the magnet, get a compass. Bring one end of the magnet near the dark end of the compass needle. The compass needle is a magnet, and the dark end is the north-seeking pole. If the dark end of the compass needle is attracted to the end of your magnet, then this end of your magnet is a south-seeking pole. You know this because two different kinds of poles will attract each other. If the dark end of the compass needle is pushed away by the end of your magnet, then this end of your magnet is a north-seeking pole. This must be so, because two of the same kinds of poles will repel, or push away, each other. Now that you know the poles of your magnet, put a big N and S with red paint on the ends of the magnet.

Make a magnet that has three poles. This magnet will have a pole at each end and one in the middle. Get a large safety pin. Be sure it is made of steel, not brass. Make a magnet out of the safety pin. You can do this by rubbing the pin with one pole of a magnet. Rub the safety pin one hundred times in the same direction. The pin will then be a magnet with two poles. Open up the pin and bend the part with the sharp point until the pin is straight. This will give you a magnet with three poles. The pointed end will be a pole, the head will be a second pole, and the middle will be a third pole. You can test the poles by picking up fine steel that has been cut up into tiny bits. Did you find out that this safety pin magnet is strongest at the middle and weakest at the ends?

Make your own permanent magnets. Get a narrow cardboard tube. The tube that comes inside a roll of paper towels will do. Use a tube that is about six inches long. If the tube is longer than six inches, cut it down to a smaller size. Wrap bell wire about 100 times around the tube. Put a nail file, steel knitting needle, sewing needle, or anything else made of steel inside the tube. Then connect the ends of the bell wire to the screws of a dry cell for just a few seconds. Be sure to take the cover off the ends of the wire first, so they are bare. Take away the wires from the dry cell, then take out the things you put into the tube. They will be permanent magnets. See if they will pick up tacks or bits of steel wool. If you use more turns of wire, or use two dry cells instead of one, your permanent magnets will be stronger.

Get a very small plastic auto with wheels that turn. Attach an iron nail with Scotch tape or friction tape to the underside of the auto. Put a drop of oil between each wheel and axle to help the auto move easily. Place the auto on a long piece of cardboard. Now hold a magnet underneath the cardboard. Move the magnet around. The auto will move without a driver.